Strategic Principles for Women in Leadership

Methods of Goal Setting and its Application in Business

Strategic Principles for Women in Leadership

Methods of Goal Setting and its Application in Business

NECOLE F. TURNER, JD

EXPECTED END

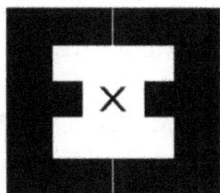

ENTERTAINMENT

Atlanta, GA

Published by Expected End Entertainment/EX3 Books
ExpectedEndEntertainment@gmail.com * www.EX3Books.com
ISBN-10: 0-9968932-8-8
ISBN-13: 978-0-9968932-8-2
Printed in the United States of America

DEDICATION

For my mother, Helen, a survivor, and my one and only sister, Katrina, I love you. To Felix, who is always my best supporter, Nicholas and Cristian the very best part of my every day, to my brothers Tuboise and Christopher, my ride and die, to Hugh and Veleria Turner, the best family ever and especially to those who served as a source of encouragement, listened to all my "dreams" and who have loved me unconditionally, I say, "Thank you."

PURPOSE OF THE BOOK

Like a lot of women, I have struggled with my career and the direction that I wanted it to go. After some heartfelt reflection, I concluded that the reason why I struggled, was because I sabotaged my goal setting. Sure, I knew how to set measurements of where I wanted to be in the next 5, 10 or even 15 years…but I had no earthly idea of how I was going to get there. I couldn't get out of my own way. So, in 2015 I made it a point to make a list of things I wanted to accomplish. Some people call this a "bucket list" but for me that seemed too morbid. I made instead what I called a "progress list" and checked them off as I completed them and in the end I amazed myself.

**Tuff Mudder Full Course (20 Obstacles in Mud and Water)

***Leaving relaxed hair behind and embracing my natural texture (The summer was brutal)

****Speaking at my first two major corporate events (Scared the living daylights out of me)

*****Transitioned into my mid 40's (Loved the freedom it gave)

******Quit My Full-Time Job (I took a leap of faith and invested in ME)

The things on this list have one thing in common.... they were all things that enhanced my growth and placed me on the path to setting higher goals. This book is for those women who endeavor to do the same. Thank you to Felix, Nicholas and Cristian who support me in my braveness everyday...love, light and blessings!

CONTENTS

INTRODUCTION xi

PART 1...

THE IMPORTANCE OF GOAL SETTING 1

PART 2...

THE ACCOUNTABILITY FACTOR................... 17

PART 3...

DIFFERENT GOAL SETTING METHODS..... 21

PART 4...

APPLY WHAT YOU'VE LEARNED.................. 39

PART 5...

WRITE THE VISION 57

PART 6...

YOUR WORK SPACE...................................... 63

ABOUT THE AUTHOR 73

INTRODUCTION

"One of the most courageous things you can do is identify yourself, know who you are, what you believe in and where you want to go."
Sheila Murray Bethel,
CEO Bethel Leadership Institute

According to a research project conducted by Leadership IQ, "Women care about their goals more than men: Women tend to develop a greater emotional connection to their goals than men. This increased heartfelt connection helps women stick to their goals when the going gets tough." However, the study also states that men do a better job of visualizing their goals and women often tend to be hard on themselves setting unattainable short-term goals AND unrealistic long term goals. This leaves a disconnect between the process of setting goals and actually obtaining them.

Historically women in many countries were not taught to take pride in setting goals for themselves. Goals are directly linked to self-value and give confidence in many other aspects of life including education. Goals are synonymous to education and employment just like peanut butter and jelly are to bread. This in turn can explain the lack of women in leadership roles. If women are not setting goals at the same pace of men; the gap, then continues to widen at the top levels in corporations. The only way we can attempt to close the gap would be by impressing the importance of goal setting among women and continuing education. This can be accomplished by modeling. Taking women who are in current leadership roles and training them on how to put into place an effective method of setting goals is what's needed to help close the gap. Modeling also can enhance the mind-set of women. For me, if I see other women who are in a position of leadership and power then naturally I feel, I can endeavor to do the same.

There are some arguments against goal setting. Adam Galinsky, a professor at Northwestern University's Kellogg School of Management, has argued that "goal setting has been treated like an over-the-counter medication when it should really be treated with more care, as a prescription-strength mediation." The argument is that placing pressure on individuals to set goals can have an adverse effect in that people will do anything to achieve them. I'm not sure how much weight this would carry with most. Conventional wisdom tells us that we should set goals at different points in life. Goals have value in that it gives a sense of pride upon their completion. Ashley Feinstein, a money coach who writes for Forbes Magazine, reinforced this by saying "the most important part of goal-setting is celebrating our successes. How will you reward yourself for hitting your benchmarks along the way? How will you celebrate once you've reached your goal? We want something that can provide us with the motivation and determination to continue to work toward it even when things don't go as planned or are more difficult than we anticipated." This in a nutshell summarizes the need to set goals.

There are three fallacies that need to be combated when it comes to women and goal setting. The following are statements that we tell ourselves or others tell us in the process:

FALLACY #1: We, as women, aren't equipped to set high level goals.

FALLACY #2: We, as women, don't really know what our goals are.

FALLACY #3: The goals set aren't aligned with the roles we've as women.

The first two fallacies are related to how we view ourselves the last is related to how others may view us. All of which are without merit and need to be debunked.

PART ONE

THE IMPORTANCE OF
GOAL SETTING

"You can and should set your own limits and clearly articulate them. This takes courage, but it's also liberating and empowering, and often earns you new respect."
Rosalind Brewer, President and CEO of Sam's Club, a division of Wal-Mart Stores Inc.

The Importance of Goal Setting

I've read that there are at least seven benefits of setting goals. According to a blog article entitled, "The Healthy Manager", they range from concepts that benefit the mind to those that benefit our relationship with others. These benefits are:

- Clearer Focus
- The Optimum Use of Resources
- Effective Use of Time
- Peace of Mind
- Clarity in Decision Making
- Freedom of Thought
- Communication with Others

"Everyone has the same amount of hours per day, it's not that you don't have enough time, it's that you don't have a clear focus"
Bridget English, Author

Clearer Focus

Many reasons exist on why people fail to achieve their goals. One of which is that they lack clarity of vision about the life they want to live. The reason for this lack of clarity is that they have committed little, or no time to developing clarity of vision. We live in an instant gratification society. The drive thru mentality not only applies to food but to our goal setting as well. I've seen this to be true with my own children.

Once my youngest broke his arm over the summer was unable to make summer workouts. When he healed, he wanted to immediately play in the first game in his regular position. Of course, this didn't happen and he was extremely disappointed. His father and I had to explain that while he was away someone else stepped in to fulfill his role. Further, if he wanted his position back he would've to work, compete and show the coaches that he was ready to return. Initially, this idea didn't make sense to him (he was 9 years old at the time) but in great spirit and gusto he took on the challenge. He knew where he wanted to be and made his focus working out and doing the work he needed to get where he wanted to be. Once this was done he regained his position in no time! Many adults think the same way about achieving goals. We want that instant gratification without a clear focus on how to get there.

"I have a low tolerance for people who complain about things but never do anything to change them. This led me to conclude that the single largest pool of untapped natural resources in this world is human good intentions that are never translated into actions."
Cindy Gallop,
Founder of If We Ran the World

Optimum Use of Resources

I can't tell you how many people that I've spoken with about goal setting. The commonality I find is that most people find it difficult to "identify" their resources. This comes from individuals not knowing what their resources are. If you aren't using your resources, you aren't being "resourceful". In business economics resources are defined "as a service or other asset used to produce goods and services that meet human needs and wants". The question then becomes how does this definition relate to goal setting? In work and in life resources can be the vehicle to help get what you want. It drives you where you want to go. It is the fuel to your end point. Think of the people that you've crossed paths, worked or volunteered with. You may have even been part of the same organization or your children in the same class at school. These are considered resources because they may have access to information that can help you complete a step in your goal setting journey. Once you master the art of optimizing your resources you'll have discovered another benefit of goal setting. People have connections and information that can benefit you. The problem is we fail to ask.

Our skills are another resource. The crux of goal setting lies in being able to identify our skills. For most of us we know what our skills are. But we get stuck when someone asks us what our "transferable skills" are in relation to career advancement. Transferable skills are the skills you acquire and move to future employment settings. Some common areas include interpersonal, communication, leadership and organizational skills.

Interpersonal Skills include: Relating, Assisting, Responding and Motivating Others.

Communication Skills include: Planning, Meeting and Following Through with deadlines. The most important in this category to me Setting and Attaining Goals.

Leadership Skills include: Managing, Evaluating and Supervising Others.

Communication Skills include: Articulating, Advising, Instructing and Persuading Others.

There are so many skills in each category but this gives you a good idea and gauge as to what you've or need to obtain.

"Nothing will work unless you do."
Maya Angelou,
Poet & Pulitzer Prize Winner

Effective Use of Time

This is an area in which I struggle with daily. I work from home and it can be easy to have gaps of time that are unaccounted for. In an age where the internet and social media is easily accessible, I found that I was spending a considerable amount of time scrolling through the latest happenings. Before I knew it half the day was gone! If I had the luxury of working for myself and from home, I would need to be more accountable with my time. The same goes for goal setting. The time you spend thinking, outlining, mapping and writing goals is directly correlated to their success. Managing distractions is one way that can make time management more effective. If you work from home, pick a time to get up each day, don't take calls for a period of time, don't turn on the television and take scheduled breaks. If you work in a busy environment, much of the same can be done. In addition to having an appointed time to check emails each day, if you minimize the distractions that lead to frustrations, the payoff will be massive. You are the vehicle to your success.

In time management, we've to find our "opportunity cost". Meaning if we're wasting valuable time in another area that won't benefit us in the long term in we're wasting a resource.... time. There's a delicate balance in finding the true value in time. It must be cultivated and respected. Remember, success doesn't drive itself, we possess the drive in us to highlight our abilities, to bring about an opportunity for success.

"Don't wait around for other people to be happy for you. Any happiness you get you've got to make yourself."
Alice Walker,
Author & Pulitzer Prize Winner

Peace of Mind

Have you ever completed a task a felt a complete sense of relief? I've been there myself and it can make the sun shine when the forecast is 100% rain. Peace of mind is a "state of mental and emotional calmness, with no worries, fears or stress". In this state, the mind is quiet, and you experience a sense of happiness and freedom. Believe or not this can be achieved in every facet of life. It's not by some mystical magical process that this occurs but by a tactful prudent approach. Goal setting does not have to be stressful. The reality is that we place more pressure on ourselves than any one external factor. What I've found in my journey is that if I "visualize" the outcome of where I want to be the process of setting goals goes a lot smoother. I mentioned earlier that men do a better job of visualizing goals. Why is this the case? Is it because women aren't capable of seeing the bigger picture? I would reason that women tend to focus on the "details" ...the little steps in between and even the obstacles that can occur. Is this the wrong approach? It's not a bad approach but there's a more effective solution. Jonathan Fields, a growth strategist, calls for us to "create a vivid picture of a specific outcome". He calls this technique "outcome simulation". Basically, we are to "visualize" the finish line before the race even starts. Athletes have often used this method when competing to hone in on their race rather than focus on the competition. Essentially, look over the horizon at where you want to be and then "map out" the steps on how to get there.

"The most difficult thing is the decision to act, the rest is merely tenacity."
Amelia Earhart,
Author & Aviator

―――――――――――

Clarity in Decision Making

The left side of our brain is the portion that houses the logical, analytical, and objective thoughts. This side of the brain is responsible for our indecisiveness. That leads to us second guessing our decisions and reasoning whether they're correct. Given that we make hundreds of decisions in any given day this can be bothersome. These decisions are the who, what and where of daily life. We've to be careful in making these decisions because we only have a certain amount of daily will power to handle these decisions. We lack self-control over the left side of our brain and this leads to total anarchy. To keep this from happening we need to make the process of decision making more concrete. To do that, we must quiet the left side of our brain. According to an article by millennial expert Ryan Jenkins, there are five keys to clear decision making, three of which are really applicable in goal setting. Getting an early start, being intentional and predetermining the expected outcome are ways to combat indecisiveness.

The morning is normally when we've the least amount of interruptions. I would also argue that this is also the time where our will power is at its highest. The previous night make a list of the items you need to accomplish. Make the list from the lowest priority to the highest. The next morning is seen as the perfect time to execute the items that are the lowest in priority. This should be done before anything else that is normally done, like responding to emails or making phone calls. This process must be intentional. Once you've completed the low priority list items move on the high priority items. This list should be small in nature. I call this the "high/low" list.

I attended a conference and the speaker mentioned that if we had more than three items on our task list everyday then we had too many. This is also true when it comes to clear decision making. Your high priority list should contain ONLY three items. Everything else needs to be pushed to the next day. This is what's meant by "predetermining" what's important to eliminate any unnecessary stress. I started thinking what are some of the things that were bringing unnecessary stress into my life? At the time, I was working a full-time job in downtown Atlanta. This required a two hour commute each day. I was married with two small children and my husband worked a full-time job that had long hours. By the time the day ended with the commute done, dinner cooked and homework completed, I was tired. The thought of getting up the next morning and doing it all again was simply exhausting. There were many times the to-do list would run through my head at day's end and I got little sleep as a result. The remedy? I had to find a balance. I had to make a short and long list of items that needed to be completed each night. Both lists only contained three items. This became my saving grace and soon I felt that I had a handle on things again. This was basically my version of the "high/low" list and it helped tremendously.

"There's a freedom in the ability to dream. There's an even greater freedom in knowing that the ability to achieve what we dream is within us."
Necole F. Turner, Author and Change Facilitator

Freedom of Thought

In high school my dream was that I wanted to be a lawyer. I remember being so excited about the idea that I had finally decided what I wanted to do with my life. It was going to be a long journey but even at that age I was committed to the task. During a visit to the guidance counselor and informing her of my plan she advised that I go into broadcast journalism instead because she did not "see me" as a lawyer. Talk about a "DREAM KILLER"!! I walked away from that session feeling defeated and second guessing myself. If it wasn't for the encouragement of a fellow classmate I might have changed my mind. Have you ever experienced someone talking you out of a plan or strategy even before it began? This can be disheartening to say the least. Most times it's not that you aren't going in the right direction. After all the ability to be completely in charge of our career path is empowering. What I've found is that the vision that others have of you is not the perception that you've for yourself. To prevent this from happening, enlist the help of others to keep motivate you. Find someone that you can trust to give you sound advisement. Also in my development of my goals I employed an acronym to help me stay on course:

> D-Determine Your Path
> R-Research the Plan
> E-Estimate the Time
> A-Articulate Your Needs
> M-Move Forward

When it's all said and done, the journey is yours alone. No one person should have the power to control the outcome. Don't spend time living within the scope of someone else's vision. Take control and commit to your process!

"Our emerging workforce is not interested in command-and-control leadership. They don't want to do things because I said so; they want to do things because they want to do them."
Irene Rosenfeld,
CEO of Mondelēz International

Communication with Others

People in general love talking about themselves. But when it comes to communicating well...that is something that is totally different. Communication in its basic form is defined as "imparting or exchanging information". But that's just on the surface. Communication when it comes to goal setting needs to be "a connection between people". In a corporate setting, it's important for the executive level to communicate effectively with their management level and so on and so on. If there's a gap, the communication isn't seen as effective. This can have a negative impact in the relaying the goals and objectives. How can this be solved?

There's a four-step approach in how managers can better communicate with other levels within the company. This method can also be applied in our personal journey. This was outlined by Jake Newfield in "How to Communicate Your Goals" in a Huffington Post blog:

1. Talk About Their Business

    Mr. Newfield recommends "Try to get an understanding of their business, their triumphs and struggles, their goals, and everything that makes them tick. Asking the right questions will get them talking and feeling more comfortable with you. Once you've a solid understanding of their position, reflect and empathize with their problems, praise their successes, and instill confidence and optimism by expressing compliments. If possible, draw commonalities between your situation and theirs, and build common ground.

2. State the Value

    In addition, he recommends "before they get bored, introduce an immediate value to them and their business. This involves finding a value before reaching out to them. This value could've an introduction, information, resources, anything. Entice them with an explicit offer of value that is tied to their current goals or efforts. Perhaps the value statement is that you possess the quality or skills They're looking for, or that you can connect them with someone in your network."

3. Connect Your Goals with Theirs

He further adds after you've completed steps one and two, a rapport is built. Then you "Introduce your goals in context with theirs. The idea is to help them realize that achieving your goals will benefit them as well. This requires creativity. If your goal is to get an introduction, figure out a way that this will benefit them, and demonstrate the value to them."

4. Call to Action

Lastly "Don't waste their time. Once you've elicited a clear path for both of you to achieve your goals, present a course of action. This needs to be easy, actionable, and measurable."

PART TWO

THE ACCOUNTABILITY FACTOR

"One of the most courageous things you can do is identify yourself, know who you are, what you believe in and where you want to go."
Sheila Murray Bethel,
CEO Global Leadership Institute

The Accountability Factor

If there are so many benefits to setting goals why is it so hard to follow through with setting them? The answer is that we lack accountability. In 2015, I joined a "Mastermind Group". This group was comprised of a group of women who were also entrepreneurs. Each woman had their own business niche and were at the top of their game. We completed a Periscope Day where each of us gave a presentation and the collaboration was wonderful. One lasting memory came from that experience and that was WE ALL held one another "accountable" for our respective role. To this day, I've partnered with one of the women to be each other's check and balance when it comes to our business goals. We've monthly check-ups to discuss our progress on old projects and celebrate any victories. Most of all we're there to help encourage and uplift one another.

Accountability is important to the process of goal setting. Most times when contemplating a major move, we keep silent. There's strength in numbers so we need to build a team of trusted individuals that help and hold us accountable. In telling others our goals it can make the goal real, helps inspire, and allows us to elicit feedback.

PART THREE

DIFFERENT GOAL SETTING METHODS

"There's nothing like a concrete life plan to weigh you down. Because if you always have one eye on some future goal, you stop paying attention to the job at hand, miss opportunities that might arise, and stay fixedly on one path, even when a better, newer course might have opened up."
Indra Nooyi,
CEO of PepsiCo

Different Goal Setting Methods

Many companies recognize that there's benefit to employees having a work life balance. Companies often seek to add work-life balance benefits because it makes good business sense. The three top reasons are the (1) recruitment/retention of employees, (2) commitment to the firm, and (3) productivity. But nothing should be more important than supporting women in their efforts in upward progression in the company. In doing so measurable outcomes must be in place to help women feel that they're a part of the corporate structure. Acknowledgement that every employee is more than a worker, recognizing that there's a 'whole person' with a life that extends outside the workplace, and demonstrates that employees' lives should be respected. This if facilitated by the organization would go a long way in fostering advancement. If there's growth in this area, then the process of goal setting will be encouraged.

Many methods exist to set goals. There's a direct correlation between our goal setting, our personal life, health and our careers. Many people find it difficult to focus on career goals if their health and personal life are out of sync. There's a mind, body and spirit connection in every facet of our lives. When there's loss of balance in one area the rest will suffer the same affliction.

ABC's Method

In a Psychology Today blog titled "Keys to Effective Goal Setting," the author emphasized that coaches should use the ABC's in teaching goal-setting techniques to individuals. The article outlined that goals should be Achievable, Believable and that there should be a Commitment to getting them completed. The effectiveness of the goal setting process, according to this model, is heavily dependent on the personalization of the goal to the individual.

1. The goal must reflect positivity.
2. The goal set must obtain a subsequent goal.
3. All the goals must ultimately lead to an outcome.

In essence, the idea is to set goals that can be completed sequentially. They need be completed in order because They're heavily dependent upon one another. One goal needs to be completed to get to the next level. The tasks would need to be completed according to their importance:

A – These are tasks you want to get done today and are the highest priority.

B – These would be nice to finish, but you'll live another day if you don't complete them.

C – Lowest priority, these tasks tend to have no sense of urgency but are nice to complete at some point.

One fallacy with this method is that if a task doesn't get completed from List A that has bearing on list B then will that impact the overall goal? Will anything ever get done? A second question is how does the rate the urgency rank in each task if They're dependent on one another? This can be a confusing process but this model can be used for some shorter-term goals I believe.

Questions and Review

   1. What are the ABC's of goal setting?

_____

_____

_____.

2. Is this way of setting goals realistic? Why or why not?

_____

_____

_____.

3. What's one common fallacy associated with this method?

_____

_____

_____.

4. What would the challenge be in using this method?

_____

_____

_____.

5. Would you use this particular method of goal setting on your journey? Please explain why.

_____

_____

_____.

SMART Method

An article in Forbes Magazine highlighted that only 15% of employees strongly agree that their goals will help them achieve great things. In addition, only 13% of employees strongly agree that their goals this year will help them maximize their full potential. Why such low percentages when it comes to the belief in our ability to accomplish goals? The article seems to suggest that setting goals that are "specific, measurable, attainable, relevant and timely" limit one's ability to "live outside of the box". In essence, people lose their ability to be free to dream bigger and do more. The method also fails to take into account the "difficulty" factors that come into play. I'm not so sure that I'm sold on the reasoning of the article and the fallacy of the argument. My thinking is we need to have a guidepost in our journey. A map to lead us to a certain destination. I may not be where I'm going to end up but I can take measurable steps to get to where I want to be. I learned the SMART Method in college when I was deciding what to do after graduation. It helped me chart a course for my life after…. for that I'm immeasurably grateful.

Specific Goals

The goal must be clear and well defined. Vague or generalized goals aren't good because they don't provide sufficient direction. You are making goals to help map out where you want to go. Remember a map is a guide to get to from point to another. We live in a day and time where GPS is the standard. However, our goals aren't automatically programmed and we're in charge of the updating of them from time to time.

Measurable Goals
    Be sure to include in your goals precise amounts, dates etc. that can be used as deadlines. If your goal is simply defined as "to obtain an IT Certification" how will you know when you've been successful? In six months or one year? Success can only be measured by its completion so set a reasonable, manageable time frame.

Attainable Goals
    You must make the goals you set reachable. Something that is within a distance that you can visualize. The goal has to be in a category of "definitely want to do" not "maybe want to do". This placement gives it an urgency instead of it being plausible. The sky is the limit when it comes to our dreams but even our dreams are limited how we categorize them.

Relevant Goals
    Our goals are vehicles to our success. That success is dependent on the goals we set. With that being said, the relevancy of them is key. This determination hinges on the goals value to your overall vision. Make the decision to align the goal with the vision and make steps to bring it fruition. You can't have a fragmented view of what you are trying to accomplish.

Timely Goals

Give yourself time enough to finish the goal(s) that you set. There's nothing more aggravating than feeling you are rushed in a task. This is a high stakes game of cards and a move in the wrong direction can delay the process. When establishing a goal, don't make it so big that you risk undermining your performance. Allow room for setbacks. If you do this frustration is less likely to set in.

Below is an example of a goal. After reading the breakdown of what the SMART Method consists of see if you can apply what you've learned.

Example:

By September 1, 2017, implement a new performance management system for use by the Executive Staff, that establishes clearly defined rules and guidelines, that will help outline for managers and employees the processes in place that can more competently evaluate performance and help develop their careers.

Questions and Review

1. What's the SMART Method of goal setting?

_____

_____

_____.

2. Is this way of setting goals relevant? Why or why not?

_____

_____

_____.

3. What's one common fallacy associated with this method?

_____

_____

_____.

4. What would the challenge be in using this method?

_____

_____

_____.

5. Would you use this particular method of goal setting on your journey? Please explain why.

_____

_____

_____.

The F.I.T. Method

The F.I.T. Method is something that I invented to help me in my journey of goal setting. It takes into account the whole person. Meaning it takes on the mental, physical and emotional parts of an individual.

This is what's called an integrative wellness approach. Integrative Wellness is defined as "using traditional and holistic approaches in helping individuals achieve desired outcomes". This approach enables individuals to address all levels of concerns in a more complete way. Essentially it gives individuals the ability to overcome habits, obstacles and patterns that have served as roadblocks in the past. With that in mind, let's examine this approach a little further.

Face Your Fears

It has often been said that the best predictor of future behavior is past behavior. When something doesn't work for us we move on to the next thing, only to take the same route. Repetition is normal anything outside of that is unfamiliar. Walking an unknown path can be downright scary. Fear of the unknown is what hinders us from going after what we truly want. In short fear is a symptom.

Synonyms of fear shed light on its application in our lives. Fear is compared to a painful agitation in the presence or in the anticipation of danger. It can also be implied to be anxiety and loss of courage. Fear in in its simplest form can cause panic that is so real as to manifest hysterical behavior as a reaction to a circumstance. Fear can show up in every aspect of our lives. When something doesn't work for us we move on to the next thing, only to take the same route. Repetition is normal anything outside of that is unfamiliar. Walking an unknown path can be downright scary. Fear of the unknown is what hinders us from going after what we truly want. Breaking this "fear" cycle is intentional and must be done to move forward in our goals. To do this, we must get to the root of the fear. Was it a disappointment that caused you to doubt your ability? Was it someone who didn't support our endeavors? Did you want something really bad and it didn't work out? All of the things mentioned can result in self-doubt. Self-doubt can lead to fear. Acknowledging past disappointment can go a long way in healing and restoring confidence.

Identify Your Passion
All of us to some degree want to be happy. Happiness is the cornerstone of having a good life. For one reason or another, "true happiness" is seen as a myth or illusory. It can evade us even with the greatest of intention. Happiness is defined as "a mental or emotional state of well-being defined by positive or pleasant emotions ranging from contentment to intense joy". A happy mental state may also reflect good or bad judgement by a person about their overall well-being. Okay, that was a lot but I want to focus on the last portion of the definition. To paraphrase "happiness reflects the way a person feels about themselves". This is true in a lot of ways. Happiness is a surface feeling that has a deeper source. There are many theories to be happy. But the most commonly agreed upon are:

1. Health and energy
   - Having a high level of health and energy is a very important component of happiness. Without health and energy, it's very difficult to feel truly and completely happy, even if you feel fulfilled in all four other categories.

2. Relationships with family and others
   - Love, companionship, and respect are very important components of happiness.

3. Meaningful work
   - Having work that is meaningful to you'll be instrumental in helping you achieve your highest level of happiness.

4. Financial freedom
   - While you don't have to be rich to be happy, being free from financial worry is very important. Being able to pay obligations and have the things you really want is important too.

5. Inner peace understanding
   - Having inner peace is crucial to happiness. Inner peace prevents the kind of turmoil that can lead to unhappiness. Once we understand the process of gaining inner peace the

process to getting there becomes easier.

Out of these five theories number three "meaningful work" is integral to the F.I.T. Method. If there's something in our lives that drives us to get up day after day AND we are excited, I would say that we're passionate about it. Our passions aren't always apparent. They don't jump out and screaming "here I am...take me...I'm available". More often than not, they are hidden deep inside. Most things we do in life are on autopilot. There's an internal clock that goes off and we start the engine. Our passions are hidden deep inside of us and need to be uncovered.

The question then becomes "how do I find my passion"? Okay, okay it may be a little cliché but the ability to "find" your passion does really exist...sort of. I like to think of it as "cultivating". The truth is we already have what we need...we just don't know it. Three VERY simple but three direct questions that we need to ask ourselves:

1. How does my work, job, career benefit me?
2. How does my work, job, career benefit other people?
3. If I were to leave this work, job, career tomorrow what's next?

Can you honestly answer all three questions completely and honestly? If not, you've got work to do. All of us have a "WHY". The reason behind our motivation. Our MOTIVATION=PASSION. Yes, all of the above... in that order.

Train Your Mind

In a Forbes Magazine article by Lisa Quast, she discusses taking "action" to develop our goals. She said that this action should take the form of "training our minds" to immediately take charge of our career planning. The taking charge should be in the form of "written action plans". These action plans need to outline immediate things that you need to do to achieve your goal. The first thing, of course, that needs to be done is to "decide what that goal is". Once a goal has been decided, the article explained that you are to write the action plan and then think of any "sub goals" that you would need. Then, for each sub-goal, write a list of actions you'll complete for the sub-goal to be achieved.

Here is an example:

Goal:

By January of next year, I'll have completed a course at my local community college in business marketing and have applied for at least three jobs or promotions:

Sub-goal:

By the end of this September, I'll have enrolled in a business marketing course at my local community college.

List of actions to achieve sub-goal:

- Action 1: Contact the local community college to find out what business marketing courses they're offering right now.
- Action 2: Find out the course fees involved, as well as everything else you'll need to enroll in the course.
- Action 3: Decide which course you'll enroll in by the end of September
- Action 4: Enroll in the course by the end of September.

The idea is that if we "train" ourselves to approach goal setting in this way our "mind" becomes "trained" to think consistently in these terms. It's a deliberate process that takes effort. Keep a notebook or journal handy to jot down ideas as they come and go back over them when time permits. One fallacy with this method of goal setting is "choice". As we've learned setting goals is a deliberate process. There's nothing that is easy about it. It takes introspection and answering some questions about what we want in life. It essentially boils down to "what we want to do" and if we will devote the time.

Questions and Review
   1. What's the F.I.T. Method of goal setting?

_____
_____
_____.

2. Is this way of setting goals realistic? Why or why not?

_____
_____
_____.

3. What's one common fallacy associated with this method?

_____
_____
_____.

4. What would the challenge be in using this method?

_____
_____
_____.

5. Would you use this particular method of goal setting on your journey? Please explain why.

_____

_____

_____.

PART FOUR

APPLY WHAT YOU'VE LEARNED

"I always did something I was a little not ready to do. I think that's how you grow. When there's that moment of 'Wow, I'm not really sure I can do this,' and you push through those moments, that's when you've a breakthrough."
Marissa Mayer,
CEO of Yahoo!

Apply What You've Learned

The most effective way to understand what we've learned is to practice. The old adage "practice makes perfect" comes to mind when thinking about goal setting. Better yet, the more we practice something it enables us to be more equipped to handle "bigger" ideas later in our journey. The best way I can help illustrate this is by using hypothetical situations. I like using this method and incorporate into my coaching practice. It's essentially taking a set of facts and outlining them in a manner that will incorporate the problem-solving process in an animated fun way. Some of the situations can range from the practical to the impractical but I feel this is a great way to apply knowledge. I learned this method from my favorite law school professor. There are fond memories of her walking into class and the first thing she would say would be "hypothetical", and all her students knew that it wasn't taking time! The key to analyzing the hypotheticals is making sure that we don't assume information or facts that aren't given unless asked to do so but to think of other factors that may not be mentioned. I want you to take this same approach while applying the concepts that have been covered so far. Let's get started!

HYPOTHETICAL #1-Mary

Mary is a mother of three and has been married to William for 18 years. The ages of Mary's children are 10, 15 and 17. Her oldest child will be graduating this year and is planning on going to college in the fall. For the last 10 years, since her last child was born, Mary has been a full time stay at home mother. During that time, she has been the cook, chauffer, concierge and event planner for her family. Prior to that she was a financial planner for a large banking institution. She has a bachelor's degree in finance and she is thinking now is the time to renter the work force since her children are getting older. She's worried however that too much time has passed and that she is not prepared to meet the challenges of working full time again. She also feels that she is rusty on her accounting skills and may need a refresher course. There's also the question of whether or not she is qualified to work in the financial industry because it has been so long since she has searched for a job. She is also concerned that working full time will take time away from her husband and children.

Based upon the above scenario answer the following questions using the following models of goal setting:

Analyze using the ABC's Model

What's the primary goal of Mary, according to this hypothetical? What are some of the challenges Mary will face making this goal "achievable"?

_____

_____

_____.

If Mary were talking with a friend, how could this goal be seen as believable?

_____

_____

_____.

Based on what you know at this time, do you think Mary will be committed to her goals?

_____

_____

_____.

Based on what you know what's the overall advantage of using this model of goal setting?

_____

_____

_____.

Analyze using the SMART Model

What's the primary goal of Mary, according to this hypothetical?

_____

_____

_____.

What are some of the challenges Mary will face making this goal "SMART"?

_____

_____

_____.

How can this goal be "measured"?

_____

_____

_____.

If Mary were talking with as a friend, would you say this goal is "attainable"?

_____

_____

_____.

Based on what you know at this time, do you think the goals of Mary are "realistically relevant"?

_____

_____

_____.

Do you think that these goals are "timely"? Why or why not?

_____

_____

_____.

Based on what you know what's the overall advantage of using this model of goal setting?

_____

_____

_____.

Analyze using the F.I.T. Model
What's the primary goal of Mary, according to this hypothetical?

_____

_____

_____.

What are some of the challenges Mary will encounter in "facing her fears"?

_____

_____

_____.

In this hypothetical "identify the passion" of Mary.

_____

_____

_____.

How can Mary "train her mind" in this process?

_____

_____

_____.

Based on what you know what's the overall advantage of using this model of goal setting?

_____

_____

_____.

HYPOTHETICAL #2-JACKIE

Jackie has worked for a major pharmaceutical company for 20 years. She loves what she does but isn't in love with the "road warrior" lifestyle any longer.

Clocking more than two plane trips a week over the last 20 years has taken a toll. Jackie is feeling a bit run down and disheartened after a recent merger with a rival company. Jackie has a Bachelor's Degree in Chemistry and a Master's Degree in Marketing. She graduated from college when she was 23 years old and has been working ever since. Her one regret is that she never got married or had any children but always figured that she would've had time for that. Having done well in her career and with a nice retirement package and savings, Jackie was able to purchase a condo and live a pretty moderate lifestyle. She is not sure what she is going to do but really is interested in being "still" for a while and maybe working from home, but she is unsure of where to look or start.

Based upon the above scenario answer the following questions using the following models of goal setting:

Analyze using the ABC's Model
What's the primary goal of Jackie, according to this hypothetical?

_____

_____

_____.

What are some of the challenges Jackie will face making this goal "attainable"?

_____

_____

_____.

If Jackie were talking with a friend, how could this goal be seen as believable?

_____

_____

_____.

Based on what you know at this time, do you think Jackie will be committed to her goals?

_____

_____

_____.

Based on what you know what's the overall advantage of using this model of goal setting?

_____

_____

_____.

Analyze using the SMART Model
What's the primary goal of Jackie, according to this hypothetical?

_____

_____

_____.

What are some of the challenges Jackie will face making this goal "SMART"?

_____

_____

_____.

How can this goal be "measured"?

_____

_____

_____.

If Jackie were talking with you as a friend, would you say this goal is "attainable"?

_____

_____

_____.

Based on what you know at this time, do you think the goals of Jackie are "realistically relevant"?

_____

_____

_____.

Do you think that these goals are "timely"? Why or why not?

_____

_____

_____.

Based on what you know what's the overall advantage of using this model of goal setting?

_____

_____

_____.

Analyze using the F.I.T. Model
What's the primary goal of Jackie, according to this hypothetical?

_____

_____

_____.

What are some of the challenges Jackie will encounter in "facing her fears"?

_____

_____

_____.

In this hypothetical "identify the passion" of Jackie.

_____

_____

_____.

How can Jackie "train her mind" when it comes to this goal?

_____

_____

_____.

Based on what you know what's the overall advantage of using this model of goal setting?

_____

_____

_____.

HYPOTHETICAL #3-NINA

Nina is a small-town girl from Tennessee. She grew up the oldest of 6 children and the product of a single parent home. In spite of all that, Nina was able to finish high school and earn a scholarship to college in Georgia. When she finished college, she went to work for a major grocery store chain. It was great because it was the same chain of stores she worked for during her summer breaks in high school. Nina worked hard and eventually made Department Head. After working in this position for a few years Nina wants to be promoted. She expresses her interest to her supervisor but does not feel encouraged by their conversation. It has been a few weeks since her conversation with her supervisor and she decides after speaking with a "trusted" co-worker to talk with human resources regarding her desires. Nina is given information on the vacancies available and what she needs "highlight" herself for promotion. Just when Nina hits her stride she receives news that her mother is ill back home. Since she is the oldest Nina must return to Tennessee to help care for her mother.

Based upon the above scenario answer the following questions using the following models of goal setting:

Analyze using the ABC's Model

What's the primary goal of Nina, according to this hypothetical?

_____

_____

_____.

What are some of the challenges Nina will face making this goal "attainable"?

_____

_____

_____.

If Nina were talking with a friend, how could this goal be seen as believable?

_____

_____

_____.

Based on what you know at this time, do you think Nina will be committed to her goals?

_____

_____

_____.

Based on what you know what's the overall advantage of using this model of goal setting?

_____

_____

_____.

Analyze using the SMART Model
What's the primary goal of Nina, according to this hypothetical?

_____

_____

_____.

What are some of the challenges Nina will face making this goal "SMART"?

_____

_____

_____.

How can this goal be "measured"?

_____

_____

_____.

If Nina were talking with as a friend, would you say this goal is "attainable"?

_____

_____

_____.

Based on what you know at this time, do you think the goals of Nina are "realistically relevant"?

_____

_____

_____.

Do you think that these goals are "timely"? Why or why not?

_____

_____

_____.

Based on what you know what's the overall advantage of using this model of goal setting?

_____

_____

_____.

Analyze using the F.I.T. Model

What's the primary goal of Nina, according to this hypothetical?

_____

_____

_____.

What are some of the challenges Nina will encounter in "facing her fears"?

_____

_____

_____.

In this hypothetical "identify the passion" of Nina.

_____

_____

_____.

Is there anything Nina can do to "train her mind" in this goal?

_____

_____

_____.

Based on what you know what's the overall advantage of using this model of goal setting?

_____

_____

_____.

PART FIVE

WRITE THE VISION

"I've learned that fear limits you and your vision. It serves as blinders to what may be just a few steps down the road for you. The journey is valuable, but believing in your talents, your abilities, and your self-worth can empower you to walk down an even brighter path. Transforming fear into freedom - how great is that?"
Soledad O'Brien,
Journalist

Write the Vision

In the above hypotheticals, we were introduced to Mary, Jackie and Nina. In the scenarios, each of them had dreams and aspirations that they were trying to accomplish. Each of them had a difficulty that was keeping them from making a decision. We then went through the process of helping them figure out the best approach using the different models of goal setting. One factor that would've made the process a bit easier for them would be if they had a clear vision of where they wanted to be. Below are some key questions to consider when articulating a vision for your goals:

- *How do you define career success? Are you achieving some level of success in your current job?*

- *What would you want to do today if all your bills were paid and you had relatively unlimited cash reserves?*
- *What would your career be like if you had the power to make it any way you wanted?*
- *If absolutely no obstacles stood in the way of your achieving it, what would you most like to attain in your career?*
- *Who are the people you most admire? What's it about them or their careers that attract you to them? Is there something about what they have or do that you want for your career vision?*
- *Do you feel as though you've a gift or calling? How can you share this gift or best answer the call in a way that will fulfill you?*
- *What's the one activity you most love? Is it part of your career? If not, how can you make it part of your career?*

The importance of having a vision is key to building purpose, intention and bringing reality to your goal setting process. The above statements really are closely akin the concept of short and long term goal setting and can be applied in your career.

Long-term career goals can be set for anything you want to achieve that is over the five-year mark. They help define where you want to go in your career. Short term career goals are those that act as a vehicle to help you get to your long term. They're usually set in one year increments but can be set on a shorter time frame especially if you are looking to gain advancement. There are a number of individuals who are adept at setting career goals. They're usually the ones who have been used to doing this since birth, but for the majority of us, myself included, struggle. I have discovered through trial and error that career goals are another version of our "desires" hence the term "desired outcome".

Goals can be written in the broad sense and in a narrower one. Examples of short-term goals include:

- *Becoming a Manager, Department Head or CEO.*
- *Making a career change, starting a second career or launching a business venture.*
- *Planning for early retirement.*

If you want to be more technical in your goals, there's sort of an art to writing them. Databasestar.com provides some great examples of "long term career goals" written for an IT Professional.

For other professions, the site below has great objectives and goal examples:
https://performancemanager.successfactors.com/doc/po/develop_employee/carguide.html

- **"Effective and experienced project manager capable of delivering multi-year projects".** This demonstrates the kind of role you want to move in to, and the level of experience or responsibility needed for it. Multi-year projects aren't simple as they take a few years to deliver.

- **"Team leader for a large team of software developers."** This could've for someone who is a software developer and wishes to move into a team leadership role, focusing on larger teams. Many skills need to be learned for this transition.

- **"Become the most knowledgeable and effective Java developer in the area."** Becoming knowledgeable is a good aspiration, and knowing the development language inside and out is a great goal to have, especially for your local area.

- **"To gain the Expert level ISTQB CTEL certification for software testing."** Getting a certification in your focus area is a common goal, but you also need to determine why you want it. This certification is for software testing, but you can rewrite it for other areas of IT.

PART SIX

YOUR WORK SPACE

"Just as my mother said, 'You can do anything if you put your mind to it, you work hard and you take that responsibility,' and I think that that would be my message."
Marillyn Hewson,
President and CEO of Lockheed Martin

Your Work Space

Now that we've learned the different approaches to goal setting. Let's take a look at what goals you BELIEVE are needed on your journey. It's time to write, edit and evaluate your next step.

Instructions: In this section, I want you to think of a goal that you've in the area of improving your **PERSONAL LIFE.**

What's your immediate goal in this area?

_____

_____

_____.

Now take this immediate goal and explain why it's important?

_____

_____

_____.

What do you need to do right now to make it happen?

_____

_____

_____.

On the scale of 1-10 how important is the goal to you and why?

_____

_____

_____.

What steps are you willing to take to make this goal a reality?

_____

_____

_____.

Now choose and circle a Model of Goal Setting (ABC'S, SMART, and F.I.T.). Then map out a plan on how to achieve this goal in the space below.

What Model of Goal Setting are you planning on using? Why?

_____

_____

_____.

After choosing your Model of Goal Setting use the steps you've learned and outline the steps to YOUR goal below.

_____

_____

_____

_____

_____

_____

_____

_____

_____

_____

_____

_____

_____

What do you believe is the most valuable concept you've learned using this Model of Goal setting?

_____

_____

_____.

Instructions: In this section, I want you to think of a goal that you've in the area of improving your **EDUCATIONAL.**

What's your immediate goal in this area?

_____

_____

_____.

Now take this immediate goal and explain why it's important?

_____

_____

_____.

What do you need to do right now to make it happen?

_____

_____

_____.

On the scale of 1-10 how important is the goal to you and why?

_____

_____

_____.

What steps are you willing to take to make this goal a reality?

_____

_____

_____.

Now choose and circle a Model of Goal Setting (ABC'S, SMART, and F.I.T.) Then map out a plan on how to achieve this goal in the space below.

What Model of Goal Setting are you planning on using? Why?

_____

_____

_____.

After choosing your Model of Goal Setting use the steps you've learned and outline the steps to YOUR goal below.

_____

_____

_____

_____

_____

_____

_____

_____

_____

_____

_____

_____

_____

_____

_____

What do you believe is the most valuable concept you've learned using this Model of Goal setting?

_____

_____

_____.

Instructions: In this section, I want you to think of a goal that you've in the area of improving your **EMPLOYMENT or CAREER.**

What's your immediate goal in this area?

_____

_____

_____.

Now take this immediate goal and explain why it's important?

_____

_____

_____.

What do you need to do right now to make it happen?

_____

_____

_____.

On the scale of 1-10 how important is the goal to you and why?

_____

_____

_____.

What steps are you willing to take to make this goal a reality?

_____

_____

_____.

Now choose and circle a Model of Goal Setting (ABC'S, SMART, and F.I.T.) Then map out a plan on how to achieve this goal in the space below.

What Model of Goal Setting are you planning on using? Why?

_____

_____

_____.

After choosing your Model of Goal Setting use the steps you've learned and outline the steps to YOUR goal below.

_____

_____

_____

_____

_____

_____

_____

_____

_____

_____

_____

_____

_____

_____

What do you believe is the most valuable concept you've learned using this Model of Goal setting?

_____

_____

_____.

ABOUT THE AUTHOR

Necole F. Turner is an author, speaker and change facilitator. Her motto of "the best thing that we've to offer is the gift of knowledge to all we encounter" is something that she applies in her everyday life. After raising her children, she struggled personally to set goals in her life and career. She then became interested in coaching other women who were seeking to re-enter the workforce after supporting their families in the home. As an Integrative Wellness Coach, she provides a holistic approach in her workshops and training of women around leadership and goal setting. She has appeared on "Atlanta Live Television" and was featured in "Atlanta's People You Need to Know Magazine" as one of the up and coming professionals in her field. She and her family reside in Atlanta.

Stay Connected with Necole
www.innovativebutterfly.com
Email: BookNecole@InnovativeButterfly.com
Facebook: Innovative Butterfly
Instagram: Innovative Butterfly
Twitter: True Butterfly

Other Works by Necole
Reflections of The Butterfly: Affirmations for Empowerment
Available at Amazon.com and www.EX3Books.com

www.ingramcontent.com/pod-product-compliance
Lightning Source LLC
Chambersburg PA
CBHW071116210326
41519CB00020B/6320